A Friend Would Say Goodbye

Written by Michol Whitney

Illustrated by Kayla Hargrove

Copyright © 2022 by Michol Whitney
Illustrations 2022 Kayla Hargrove

All rights reserved. No part of this book may be reproduced in any form or by any means without written permission from the publisher, except brief quotes for the purpose of a review.

Write2readright.com

ISBN 978-1-7364005-8-6 (hardcover)
ISBN 978-1-7364005-9-3 (paperback)

Printed in the U.S.A.

Michol Whitney
Chicago, Illinois

Mr. Zane lives next door to me.
He is a friendly neighbor.
He lets me plant in his backyard,
we put in lots of labor.

It has been a while since I have seen him.
His garden is growing wild.
His mailbox keeps getting way too full, and his papers are in a pile.

His son comes by to cut the grass.

He keeps it nice and neat.

He is no good at gardening,

but it's no easy feat.

His daughter comes to see him,

but he is never, ever there.

His house is dark and empty

and he is never in his chair.

One day while I was playing,
a crowd gathered at his house.
I watched them talk and laugh,
but I was quiet as a mouse.

Mommy walked up behind me
and she began to speak,
"There is something I must tell you,
that I have known about all week.

The news I have will sadden you
but I must keep it real.
Afterward, take a moment
and please tell me how you feel.

Mr. Zane died of COVID.
He met his untimely demise.
This was unexpected and took
his family by surprise.

His son and daughter are hurting.
They are feeling really sad.
They are trying to hang in there,
but they really miss their dad.

We will miss him too.
A better neighbor we won't find.
He was a wonderful man,
always generous and kind.

Death is very permanent,
but his memories will remain.
He has gone away for good,
but he is free of pain."

I had no words to tell my mom
to say just how I felt.
But deep inside my body
my heart began to melt.

Mommy watched and waited,
but I couldn't say a thing.
Then all at once, I cried
like a bird that had to sing.

"How could he just abandon
all the plants he loved and grew?
Did he just forget them?
Did he forget about me too?"

"Nova," Mommy said,
as she wiped away my tears,
"He did not forget you.
You've been friends for many years."

"I know," I said with confidence,
"but a friend would say goodbye.
They would never leave you hanging!
They would never make you cry!"

Mommy said, "I'm sure he would have
told you if he knew the time was near,
but death is unpredictable
and COVID is severe.

It is perfectly alright for you
to feel a need to mourn.
Crying is what you did a lot
since the day that you were born.

Learning you've lost a loved one
can be uncomfortable and strange.
People will react differently
with emotions from every range.

Lots of people cry and weep.
Grief is a natural feeling.
Other people laugh with joy,
it helps speed up the healing.

There is no protocol
to express how we show grief.
You have to do what is best for you
to give your heart relief.

The most important thing of all
is that you must reveal
how the death of someone
is affecting how you feel.

It is hard to understand
the plans for Mr. Zane.
He had a good life
and his legacy will remain.

Let us pull ourselves together.
Let us take a good, deep breath.
Because it is never easy
when you must deal with death."

"I am never going to die!
Life is way too fun to leave.
I am going to live forever,
and this you can believe.

I will always be here
and never go away.
Home is where the heart is
so it is here that I will stay."

"I'm afraid it doesn't work like that.
Although it might be nice,
but death is something special
so, consider my advice.

I am going to go away one day
and daddy will do the same.
If we stayed here forever,
then that would be a shame.

Our time here is temporary.
So make the most of every minute.
We should live our lives
like we are in it to win it.

Remember, little Nibbles,
you loved him a great deal.
You laughed as you watched him
play on his running wheel.

Until the day that he stopped
and we had no idea why.
We later found out he was sick
and it was his time to die.

You did not want him sick.
It made you sad to see him hurting.
He was so uncomfortable.
His sounds were disconcerting.

You cried for days and days
as you put him down to rest,
but deep down inside,
you knew that this was for the best.

You knew he had stopped hurting.
He was not tired anymore.
This helped you to move on
to live life just like before.

Just like little Nibbles,
Mr. Zane loved to see you smile.
They both knew that being gloomy
was not part of your style.

Mr. Zane wants you to be happy.
He does not want you feeling down.
Mr. Zane would not like knowing
that your smile is now a frown.

Don't think of how you miss him.
Don't keep wishing he was near.
Think of all the good things
that he did when he was here."

We went to see his family
to pay our last respect.
I used this time to daydream,
wonder and reflect.

His garden was so messy.
Weeds were everywhere,
but strangely, a flower was growing
to show me it was there.

"Look, Mommy!" I showed my mother.
"This flower should not be here.
The weeds will come and destroy it.
They are growing awfully near."

Mommy smiled.
"The flower does belong here.
Maybe it is a gift for you.
Maybe this is his goodbye
to say he loves you too.

Life is a funny thing
and all good things come to an end,
but he did not forget to say goodbye
to his good friend."

I appreciate this gift of life
and will cherish it every day.
I will make the most of it
in an extraordinary way.

www.ingramcontent.com/pod-product-compliance
Lightning Source LLC
Chambersburg PA
CBHW051320110526
44590CB00031B/4421